GOOD]

by

Dr. Fuller

A Series of Therapeutic
Children's Books
for Adults and Kids

DEDICATION

**To Tucker,
whose blue eyes
twinkle
with
tranquil peace
and
joyful curiosity.**

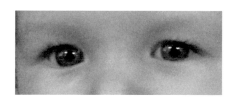

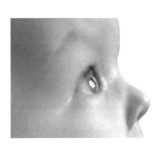

Goodbye, panic,
Goodbye, fear.
Goodbye, faintness.
Goodbye, numbness;
Goodbye, bad feelings.

Goodbye, anxiety.
Goodbye, *What if?*
Goodbye, fear.

That something awful *might* happen.
A rock and hard place,
it is not.
The bad thing won't happen!
Stop it!
I will settle down.

Just a little time . . .
I'm going to do something fast . . .

They say **I** can --
Find my balance.

Ground myself.
See safety.
Anchor my emotions.

My little friend calms me.

Be comfortable
 with who I am.

I've got the time.

I've got the tools.

I've got the control.
I've got the peace.
I've got the power.

I hear the music.

Take a deep breath or two
or three . . .

Goodbye, Tizzy and Dizzy.
Goodbye, *whatever*
sensation.

Peace from slow,
refreshing breathing.

Why not . . .
Ride right through it.
Why not . . .

Let myself relax.
With each breath out,
I feel calmer and calmer.
More and more relaxed.

Stare at the wall . . .
Goodbye, choking sensation.
Fresh breath comes.
My sight begins to blur.
Breathe easy.

Blurred vision brings calm.
Easy breathing calms me.

Count the items on the wall . . .

Goodbye, racing heart.
Fear does not count.
Now my heart finds its safe,
calm peace.

Let a deep breath out . . .
Goodbye, labored breathing.
I rock a little.

My chest settles down.

Placing hands on my thighs . . .
Goodbye, trembling --
Hello, my warm fuzzy goat.
Warmth feels so good.
Warm fond memories.

Tranquil peace and curiosity.

Close my eyes . . .
See the wall again in my mind's
eye . . .

Goodbye worry –
Go,
Vanish.
My eyes are closed –
No worry.

Look around the room . . .
Really see my world.

The clock, The poodle, The shelf,
The picture . . .

The bird.

The pillow,
The door,
The chair,
The bowl,
The floor,
The violin,

And more . . .

My calm doubles.
I'm in control . . .
Of my calming mind.

My heart rate slows.
Lub-dub, Lub-dub, Lub-dub.
A calm sigh!
Feel my deep breaths in and out.

My warm still hands.
Better, I'm better,
Even better . . .

I own my own mind.

I tell myself what to think.

Healthy!

Free!

Strong!

I soar!

I trust myself!

Safe!

Read.
Repeat.
Review.

Recite. Until you are calm.

A special thank you to Jane Bussom, who is the creator of Nannette, the warm fuzzy goat.

Sincere appreciation to Cadence Kidwell who is the guardian angel of Nannette and who provides a home to Nannette at her shop "Fuzzy Goat" at 223 West Jackson Street, Thomasville, Georgia.

http://fuzzygoatyarns.com

Notes:

Made in the USA
Columbia, SC
28 September 2024

42855613R00020